The Organic Systems Framework

The Organic Systems Framework

A New Paradigm for Understanding and Intervening in Organizational Life

Barry Oshry

Published in 2019 by:
Triarchy Press
Axminster, England

info@triarchypress.net
www.triarchypress.net

Copyright © Barry Oshry, 2019

The right of Barry Oshry to be identified as the author of this work has been asserted by him in accordance with the Copyright, Designs and Patents Act, 1988.

No part of this publication may be reproduced, stored in a retrieval system or transmitted in any form or by any means including photocopying, electronic, mechanical, recording or otherwise, without the prior written permission of the publisher.
All rights reserved

ISBN: 978-1-911193-61-6
Epub ISBN: 978-1-911193-62-3
PDF ISBN: 978-1-911193-63-0

in memory of Kurt Lewin

There is nothing so practical as a good theory

Contents

Summary 9
A visit to my local bookstore 11
There is no new paradigm 13
Pre-paradigm endless possibilities 15
A proposed candidate for paradigm status 17
The elements of the Organic Systems Framework 19
Whole organic systems as patterns of systemic relationship ... 21
Whole organic systems as patterns of system processes 27
Scenarios resulting from blindness to system processes 35
The patterns we fall into shape our consciousness 39
Understanding the root of our experiences 41
OSF as a paradigm candidate 43
Does anyone really care about scientific paradigms? 47
Summary of the Organic Systems Framework 51
References 53
About the Author 57
About the Publisher 59

Summary

The object of this booklet is twofold:

1. to establish that despite the frequent references to paradigms and paradigm shifts in the management and organization literature, there are no scientific paradigms as Thomas Kuhn has described in his landmark essay.

2. to make the case for the Organic Systems Framework (OSF) being a legitimate candidate for paradigm status, one from which research that extends, elaborates, tests, and applies the framework follows naturally.

A visit to my local bookstore

This story began in 2000 with a visit to my local bookstore. I was there with my granddaughter, our primary business being to find a book for her. As she rummaged through the shelves of the Young Adult Section, my eye caught a book lying by itself on an adjacent countertop: Thomas Kuhn's *The Structure of Scientific Revolutions* (1962).

Though I'd never read the book, I had heard it referenced in countless conversations regarding one or another new approaches to organizational life; everywhere you turned there was talk of 'new paradigms'. Kuhn's book just had no business being where it was. This was neither the Science nor the Philosophy Section; its nearest neighborhood was the Young Adult Section, and I could not envision my granddaughter or any of her compatriots being engrossed by Kuhn, at this stage of their lives at least. So, what was this book doing there? I leaned on the counter and began to read. After a few gasps and Wows! it was clear: The book was there for me.

There is no new paradigm

Despite the obligatory references to Thomas Kuhn's work, there is probably no field that talks more about – yet knows less about – scientific paradigms and paradigm shifts (as Kuhn uses the terms) than this field of management, management theory, organization development, systems thinking and so forth.

In this field, paradigm is most often used to refer to some new way (generally the author's) of looking at management, leadership or other aspects of organization life; and proposals for paradigm shifts – from hierarchy to self-directed, from patriarchy to matriarchy – seem to be based less in science than in theology or politics. My intention here is not to denigrate such contributions, which I believe are extremely valuable in stimulating thinking about organizational life… but to distinguish them from science.

In science, paradigms share two essential characteristics:

(i) the achievement of the creator of the paradigm "was sufficiently unprecedented to attract an enduring group of adherents away from competing modes of scientific activity" and

(ii) the new paradigm "was sufficiently open-ended to leave all sorts of problems for the redefined group of practitioners to resolve". (Kuhn 1962, p.10)

"Normal science" is what is carried on within the paradigm. Kuhn defines it as, "Research firmly based upon one or more scientific achievements, achievements that some particular scientific community acknowledges for a time as supplying the foundation for its further practice." (Ibid.)

Is there such an acknowledged foundation in our field? I think not. On the subject, Kuhn says, "…it remains an open question what parts of social science have yet acquired such paradigms at all." He goes on to say, "History suggests that the road to a firm research consensus is extraordinarily arduous." (Ibid. p.15)

Citing examples from electricity, heat, motion, statics, chemistry and geology, Kuhn describes a **pre-paradigm stage** in which "early fact-gathering is a far more nearly random activity ...in the absence of a paradigm or some candidate for paradigm, *all of the facts that could possibly pertain to the development of a given science are likely to seem equally valid.*" (Ibid., emphasis added.) Given the diversity and non-connectedness of the many books in this leadership, management and organization field, 'pre-paradigm' seems to be a fairly apt description.

Pre-paradigm endless possibilities

In the absence of a paradigm, there is room for every point of view. When I first studied popular management books, I found that the field imported from sports (*Sacred Hoops* by Phil Jackson, *The Winner Within* by Pat Riley, *Success is a Choice* by Rick Pitino), from Buddhism *(The Tao of Leadership* by John Heider, *Tao at Work* by Stanley Herman, *Tao of Management* by Robert Messing), from physics (*Leadership and the New Sciences* by Margaret Wheatley), from religion (*Jesus, CEO* by Laurie Jones), from popular culture (*Leadership Lessons from Star Trek: The Second Generation*), and the metaphorical possibilities appear limitless (swim with the sharks, roar with the lions, teach the elephants to dance).

My very limited research was sufficient to make the point for me; in fairness, however, I entered with the point already established. I leave it to young researchers (or beleaguered graduate students) with more patience and more taste for the variety, to study this field more systematically. For me, Kuhn's point was well demonstrated: There is no new scientific paradigm; in fact, there was no old one from which a new one could have diverged.

A proposed candidate for paradigm status

For the longest time I have felt that the Organic Systems Framework I have developed *is* solid science. By contrast, our organizational development field, as reflected in the popular literature, is modernistic, prone to staying on the surface of matters, keeping up with latest 'hot' topic, and too often leaping from fad to fad; and it is a field that demands immediate practical results. Neither tendency lends itself to serious science.

The Organic Systems Framework has evolved gradually out of my experience over the past 40 years with what at various times has been referred to as the Power & Systems Laboratory, the Power Lab, the Power & Leadership Conference, and Power Camp (Oshry 1999). Over these 40 years my colleagues and I have been able to observe a multitude of multi-class whole systems live out their existence. In each case we had the rarest of opportunities to see systems both from the **outside** – seeing the structure and processes of the whole – and from the **inside** – listening to the experiences of members within these systems. These direct observations are the foundation of the Organic Systems Framework.

I believe that OSF has matured to the point that it can be considered as a serious candidate for scientific paradigmatic status, and I am proposing it as a candidate based on the following Kuhn criteria:

a) that it is descriptive and predictive

b) that it offers improved solutions to existing social system problems

c) that it opens up broad avenues for future research.

The Organic Systems Framework does not pretend to be exhaustive – which is neither a requirement nor even a desired condition for a scientific paradigm. It *is* an encompassing framework that sets the stage for what Kuhn refers to as "normal science", aspects of which include extending, correcting and refining the theory, and testing its applications.

The elements of the Organic Systems Framework

1. **Seeing human systems as organic wholes.** OSF fits in and complements the field of general systems theory in which "a system has come to mean an integrated whole whose essential properties arise from the relationships between its parts [*and the processes of the whole*], and 'systems thinking,' the understanding of a phenomenon within the context of a larger whole." (Capra 1996 – the phrase in italics is my addition.)

    OSF meets this enlarged definition; it has a language for describing systems as wholes; and it is a framework that allows us to understand and influence the widest range of system phenomena: how, as system members, we experience ourselves, our relationships with others, the systems we are a part of, other systems, and the relationships among systems; and it allows us to take more informed actions based on these experiences.

2. **The structure and processes of the whole.** In OSF, we describe the whole as a **pattern of systemic relationships** (what the whole *is*) and as a **pattern of systemic processes** (what the whole *does*).[1]

    These are explored further in **Whole Organic Systems as Patterns of Systemic Relationship**, starting on p.21, and in **Whole Organic Systems as Patterns of Systemic Processes**, starting on p.27.

---

[1] These are described more fully in my *Seeing Systems; Leading Systems* (Oshry 1995); and, more recently, in *Context Context Context* (Oshry 2017).

Whole organic systems as patterns of systemic relationship

Patterns of systemic relationships

We have identified three key systemic relationships that determine essential properties of whole organizational systems:

Top/Bottom

End/Middle/End

Provider/Customer

These patterns of systemic relationship exist *at all levels and in all types of social systems – family, sports team, work unit, school and university faculty, organization, and nation*; and they exist in hierarchical and non-hierarchical systems. We, *regardless of our designated roles or positions*, are constantly moving in and out of these relationships, sometimes on one side, sometimes on the other.

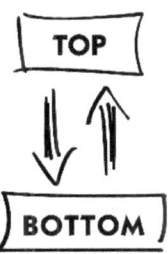

We are in a Top/Bottom systemic relationship whenever one individual or group (Top) has *designated* responsibility for some project or process, and other individuals or groups (Bottom) are members in that project or process. In some interactions we are Top, in others Bottom.

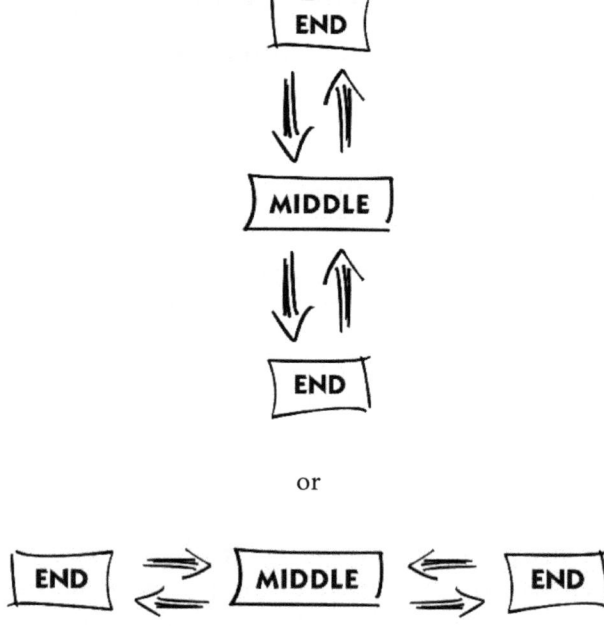

or

We are in an End/Middle/End systemic relationship whenever two or more individuals or groups with conflicting agendas, needs, desires or priorities (Ends) are looking to an individual or group (Middle) to support their agenda, needs, desires, or priorities. In some interactions we are Middle, in others we are one of two or more Ends.

We are in a Provider/Customer systemic relationship whenever one individual or group (Customer) is looking to another individual or group (Provider) to provide them with products or services. Again, in some interactions we are Provider, in others Customer.

Scenarios resulting from Blindness to system relationship

In our moment-to-moment interactions we see ourselves interacting person to person; *we do not see ourselves in systemic relationships*. As a consequence of that system blindness, there is a pattern that develops with some regularity: *the experience of responsibility for the business of the relationship* regularly flows:

- from Bottom to Top. Bottom experiences Top as responsible for the work of this relationship, and Top feels responsible.
- from Ends to Middle. Ends experience Middle as responsible for resolving Ends' issues, and Middle feels responsible.
- and from Customer to Provider. Customer experiences Provider as responsible for delivery, and Provider feels responsible.

This imbalance in *experienced* responsibility happens without awareness or choice. It is simply crystal clear in the moment that Top, Middle, and Producer are responsible and that Bottom, Ends, and Customer are not.

If Top, Middle, and Provider deliver satisfactory results, there is no apparent immediate problem[2], but should they fail, a familiar scenario of stress, negative evaluations of one another, and diminished contributions unfolds:

- Burdened Tops interacting with Oppressed Bottoms
- Weak and Torn Middles interacting with Disappointed Ends
- Righteously Done-to (Screwed) Customers interacting with Unfairly Judged Providers.

All parties tend to be blind to how these scenarios have unfolded.

---

[2] In the long run, if these patterns persist, there is likely to be a gradual disabling of both parties. See *Seeing Systems, Act II, Scene 2* in (Oshry 2007).

Our consciousness is a consequence of the relationship patterns we fall into

By 'consciousness' I mean the way that system members experience themselves, others, their system, and other systems. The responsibility patterns that I have just described and that we blindly and reflexively fall into shape our consciousness. Oppressed Bottoms *see* ineffective Tops. Disappointed Ends *see* weak ineffective Middles. Righteously Done-To Customers *see* ineffective non-responsive Providers. These experiences are felt to be accurate reflections of *reality*. This is who these others *really* are. Through the lens of the OSF, however, we recognize these experiences as the *consequences* of the patterns we have fallen into. Change the patterns, and the OSF predicts that different experiences will likely emerge.[3]

The personal bias

The OSF challenges us to overcome the personal bias by which individual, organizational, and societal breakdowns are reflexively explained as personal rather than systemic. Furthermore, since the diagnoses are personal, so too are the suggested remedies: fix, fire, rotate, separate, divorce, or provide therapy for one or more of the parties. The OSF also challenges us to overcome the personal bias in the remedies we propose. It's not that personal characteristics play no part; rather it's that viewing situations through the OSF lens provides better understanding of situations and better action strategies.[4]

---

[3] See (Oshry 2017) where the transformative changes in behavior, relationships, and contribution are described in detail.

[4] (Oshry 2010) illustrates the limitations of personal explanations and also shows the superior diagnostic and action implications provided by the OSF lens.

From blindness to awareness and choice

With the awareness that the OSF provides, it becomes possible to recognize when we are in systemic relationships *as we are living them*, and to transform these relationships with more satisfying and productive outcomes for ourselves, our relationships, and our systems.

The potential for change comes from

1. noticing the systemic relationship we are in
2. noticing where responsibility is residing and the consequences that pattern is having for us, our experience of the other, and the system
3. choosing to maintain the pattern as is or to work at changing the responsibility pattern.[5]

---

[5] Changing a systemic relationship can still be a challenging process. See (Oshry 2007).

Whole organic systems as patterns of system processes

Patterns of process: what the whole *does*

We have also identified four fundamental whole organizational system processes with which organic systems interact with their environments. These processes occur in *all* organic systems. What differentiates one system from another is the balance of these processes and the intensity and mindfulness with which they are expressed.

The patterns of process that systems fall into shape how system members experience one another, their system, and other systems. And these patterns have consequences for the ability of these systems to achieve their potential.[6]

The four processes are:

Individuation and **Integration**
and **Differentiation** and **Homogenization**.

Once again, these processes occur at all levels of systems.

Survival processes

Each of these processes has its unique potential contribution to the survival of the whole, *and* each diminishes system survivability when one predominates while other processes are suppressed.

---

[6] For a more complete explication of these processes see (Oshry 2018).

1. Whole Systems Individuate

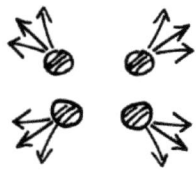

Individuation is the process in which parts of a whole system – members and groups – function independently of one another. Individuation is:

- Freedom
- Separateness
- Independence
- Responsibility for self
- The pursuit of individual goals, interests, and agendas

Survival process
Individuation strengthens the whole by turning individuals and groups free to pursue their dreams, to compete, and to contribute. (Think of the dynamics underlying free enterprise systems.)

Yet individuation without integration creates system vulnerability: chaos, inequality, actions based in self-interest resulting in damage to the system's environment (e.g. financial collapse and environmental degradation).

2. Whole Systems Integrate

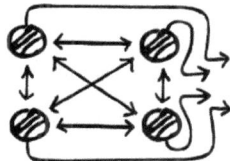

Integration is the process in which members function as parts, operating as components in service of the whole. Integration is:

- Connectedness
- Interdependence
- Mutual support
- Mutual responsibility
- Teamwork
- The pursuit of collective interests, goals, and agendas

Survival process
Integration contributes to system survival by mobilizing individuals and groups to work together in the service of common goals.

Yet integration without individuation crushes member spirit and initiative and reduces the quality of the system's products, services, and contributions.

3. Whole Systems Differentiate

Differentiation is the process by which the whole develops variety in form and function as it engages with its environment. Differentiation is:

- Variety
- Change
- Being all it can be
- Adaptability
- Richness

Survival process
Differentiation contributes to system survival by providing the whole with a variety of structures and processes for coping with the dangers in the system's environment and prospecting among its opportunities.

Yet differentiation without homogenization leads to destructive territoriality in organizations, tribalism in society, and imperialism and warfare among nations.

4. Whole Systems Homogenize

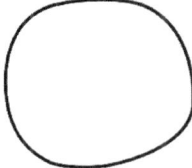

Homogenization is the process in which system information and capacity are distributed across the system. Homogenization is:

- Commonality
- Oneness
- Common knowledge
- Shared information
- Common language
- Mutual understanding

Survival process

Homogenization contributes to the survival of the whole by spreading system knowledge/information throughout the system, thereby reducing the vulnerability of the system to loss or incapacity of individuals or groups.

Yet homogenization without differentiation limits the system's capacity for coping with the dangers in the system's environment and prospecting among its opportunities.

Whole systems exert their **Power** by individuating and differentiating

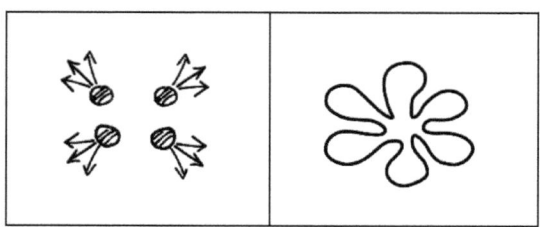

Individuation and differentiation working together are the system's high-energy **Power** processes: freedom, independence, change, the pursuit of self-interest. The potential for members and the whole to be all that they can be.

Whole systems express their **Love** by integrating and homogenizing

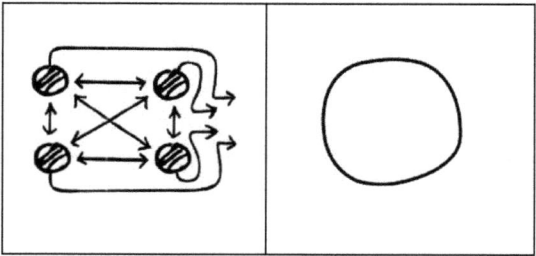

Integration and homogenization working together are the system's **Love** processes: connectedness, commonality, mutual responsibility, unity, equality, working together for common goals.

System Power processes turn us loose,
System Love processes bring us together.

System Power heats up the system,
System Love calms it down.

System Power unleashes competition,
System Love supports cooperation.

Through System Power we elaborate our differences,
Through System Love we focus on our commonalities.

Through System Power we operate independently of one another,
Through System Love we function interdependently.

Power *and* Love

All systems – families, organizations, neighborhoods, countries, the world – have the potential to be systems of Power *and* Love. As such, they more fully utilize the potential of their members; this results in more satisfying and productive relationships throughout the system, and they conduct the system's business more creatively and productively. However, in our blindness to system processes, Power and Love systems are a possibility too rarely achieved.

Scenarios resulting from blindness to system processes

In our moment-to-moment interactions, we do not see the whole systems of which we are a part, nor do we see the processes our systems are engaging in while they react to their *immediate* environments. As a result, there are patterns that recur with regularity.

Certain adaptive processes predominate while other *valuable* processes are neglected. The resulting imbalanced patterns cause personal stress for system members, broken relationships, lost opportunities, and diminished system effectiveness and contribution. All of this happens without awareness or thought.

What follows are examples of how the scenario plays out with some regularity in three organizational systems-within-systems: Top, Middle, and Bottom systems.[7]

1. Territorial Tops: Falling into Power without Love

Top systems are systems-within-systems whose members have collective responsibility for the larger system of which they are a part – top executives for the organization, project leader for the project team, parents for the family, and so on. Top systems exist in immediate environments of varying degrees of complexity, accountability, and uncertainty.

Top systems, as a way of coping with these conditions, reflexively *adapt* by differentiating and individuating – individuals and groups take on responsibility for pieces of the complexity. That in itself is not a problem, but, without

---

[7] For a more complete picture of these scenarios, see (Oshry 2017).

awareness or choice, differentiations gradually devolve into territories.

Without paying corresponding attention to homogenization and integration, the top system falls into a pattern of *Power without Love*, resulting in territorial issues among Tops, negative consequences for them personally, their relationships with one another, and the quality of their contribution to the system for which they are top.

2. Alienated Middles: Falling into Neither Power nor Love

Middle systems are systems within the larger system of the organization – middle management peer groups, department heads, supervisory groups, division heads, staff groups, and all other organizational groups whose members' primary responsibility is leading, managing, coaching or otherwise servicing other individuals or groups.

Middle systems exist in a tearing environment, one that pulls middles away from one another and out toward other individuals and groups.

The Middle system *adapts* to its tearing environment by individuating – dispersing away from one another and out toward those other individuals and groups.

Without awareness or choice, individuation gradually devolves into isolation.

Without paying corresponding attention to integration (differentiation and homogenization become irrelevant so long as there is no integrated whole which could differentiate) the middle system falls into a pattern of *neither Power nor Love* – a pattern that weakens individual members, decreases the quality of their leadership or service to others, and diminishes the effectiveness and contribution of the middle system to the whole of which it is a part.

3. Oppressed Bottoms: Falling into Love internally, and Power externally

Bottom systems are systems within the larger system of the organization whose members feel vulnerable to the decisions the Top system takes that affect their lives in major and minor ways. The Bottom system exists in an environment of real or perceived danger.

The Bottom system *adapts* to this environment by integrating and homogenizing internally (members becoming unified and uniform), and by individuating and differentiating in relation to the rest of the system (members becoming increasingly different and separate from them). Without awareness or choice, the Bottom system devolves into a *Love without Power* system internally, resulting in pressures toward conformity and suppression of individuality and dissent.

The Bottom system also devolves into *a Power without Love* system externally, resulting in resistance, passivity, disengagement, and rebellion.

All of which results in stress within and across organizational lines, broken relationships, lost opportunities, diminished contribution of members, and diminished effectiveness and contribution of the system as a whole.

The patterns we fall into shape our consciousness

The patterns Top, Middle, and Bottom systems blindly and reflexively fall into shape the consciousness of system members. Very different mentalities and relationship issues develop in each of these systems.

'Mine' mentality at the Top
Tops, in their *Power without Love* pattern, fall into a 'Mine' mentality: members becoming defensive and protective of *their* territories; there are tensions among Tops regarding issues such as the relative importance of members, lack of respect for contributions, lack of trust, lack of support. All of which has negative consequences for relationships among members of the Top system and for the system as a whole.

'I' mentality in the Middle
Middles, in their *neither Power nor Love* pattern, fall into an 'I' mentality: members, in their separateness, feel unique, feel they have little in common with one another, become judgmental of one another and competitive with one another, and feel that there is no collective power among them.

'We/Them' mentality at the Bottom
Bottoms, in their *Love without Power* pattern internally and their *Power without Love* pattern externally, fall into a 'We/Them' mentality – experiencing the goodness and righteousness of their own group members and the maliciousness, incompetence, and insensitivity of the others.

Understanding the root of our experiences

In our blindness to system processes, these scenarios with their resulting tensions, pressures, and breakdowns, all feel specific to our group and our particular circumstances. With the OSF, however, we understand these are regularly recurring patterns in Top, Middle, and Bottom systems.

In our blindness, the perceptions, feelings and judgments we have about ourselves and others are experienced as solid reflections of reality. *This is who we and they really are.* With the OSF we understand that these perceptions, feelings, and judgments are a consequence of the patterns our systems have fallen into and not the cause.

In our blindness, the solution to our issues and dilemmas is seen to be personal: fix, fire, rotate, marginalize, ignore, expel, or propose therapy for one or more of the parties. With the OSF, we understand instead that:

- life in the Top system can be transformed if Tops work at infusing Love – integration and homogenization – into Power

- life in the Middle system can be transformed if Middles work at making integration a regular part of their existence, and then see where that initial step takes them

- life in the Bottom system can be transformed if Bottoms work at unleashing member energy by infusing Power – individuation and differentiation – internally, and Love – integration and homogenization – into their interactions with the others.[8]

---

[8] See (Oshry 2017) for the challenges and opportunities that the transformative processes raise.

Through the OSF, members' experiences of one another are understood as the *consequences* of the patterns their systems have blindly and reflexively fallen into and not as reflections of reality. This is a hard pill for people to swallow, especially if their feelings have built up over time and are intense. Yet the OSF predicts that if members of these systems work together to change the patterns their systems have fallen into – bring the suppressed processes into play – there is likely to be a transformative shift in their experiences.

The politicization of whole system processes

In the absence of OSF, neutral processes are politicized. For example, to the ideologists of 'free' societies, individuation and differentiation become the valued processes, and integration and homogenization the disvalued ones (socialism, communism). Whereas to the ideologists of 'communist' societies, integration and homogenization are the valued processes and individuation and differentiation the disvalued ones (selfishness, greed). In both cases, politicized systems overvalue their core processes, and weaken themselves by denying the needed balance provided by their demonized counterparts.

Through the lens of the OSF, the societal task becomes one of understanding and managing system processes.

OSF as a paradigm candidate

The following are reasons for proposing OSF as a prime paradigm candidate:

1) OSF offers better explanations

OSF explains system phenomena better than competing models. It resolves those "recognized anomalies whose characteristic feature is their stubborn refusal to be assimilated to existing paradigms." (Kuhn 1996)

One such anomaly is the regularity with which certain interpersonal relationship patterns and breakdowns occur *independently of the personality characteristics of system members,* and *independently of the content of their systems.* Examples are the regularly occurring territoriality (turf warfare) among Tops, alienation (dis-integration) of Middle peers, and groupthink (pressures toward conformity) among Bottom peers, and We/Them relationships with non-group members. *Person-oriented and situational-oriented frameworks cannot explain these regularities; OSF does.* (Oshry 2010)

2) OSF offers improved solutions

The OSF explanations of these phenomena point to improved strategies for problem solutions. Rather than offer personal solutions (fix, fire, rotate, therapize the parties), OSF helps parties see and master the system conditions that are shaping their relationships.

With regard to systemic relationships, this means shifting the locus of responsibility in the Top/Bottom (T/B), End/Middle/End (E/M/E), or Provider/Customer (P/C) relationships.

With regard to system processes, this means adjusting the balance or intensity of processes: individuation, integration, differentiation or homogenization.

3) **OSF offers broad avenues for future research**

The research that has led to the development of OSF has been largely, though not exclusively, limited to our observations of Power Lab and Organization Workshop interactions over the past 40+ years. These have been our opportunities to stand outside systems, see them as wholes, and eventually begin to see them as patterns of systemic process and patterns of systemic relationship. As significant as these breakthroughs have been, we see them as only the beginning of understanding the full possibilities of OSF.

Once one chooses to work within the OSF paradigm, unlimited research opportunities open up, both for uncovering additional patterns of relationship and process, and for elaborating, testing and applying the model. These opportunities include:

- **Evaluate the relationship, not the person**

The process of performance evaluation is one example of a research and application direction that follows from seeing systems as patterns of relationship. The flaws of person-centered performance evaluation are clearly revealed: one party in the relationship being evaluated negatively by the other (generally a failing Bottom, Middle or Provider) *rather than having both parties evaluate how they are managing their systemic relationship*. When one sees systems as patterns of relationship, then the appropriate task becomes one of assessing how well we are managing our T/B (or E/M/E or P/C) relationship. The systemic alternative: *Evaluate the relationship, not the person.*

- **Relationship research**

More broadly, OSF proposes theory-based strategies and predicted outcomes (creating partnership) by shifting responsibility in the three systemic relationships. However, no systematic research has been done in studying the shape and consequences of existing patterns, or studying the strategies and consequences of changing strategies, i.e., *how* one creates shared responsibility in T/B, E/M/E, and P/C relationships and the *consequences* of such shifts. Broad avenues of research are available here. There may be other systemic relationships waiting to be discovered; the beseecher/besought relationship has recently been raised as a promising candidate.

- **Peer research**

In the same vein, OSF offers broad strategies and predicted outcomes for preventing or repairing breakdowns in relationships among Top peers, Middle peers, and Bottom peers.

Again, to the best of our knowledge, no systematic research has been done in studying existing patterns of process in these systems and the consequences of these existing processes, or strategies for changing processes (helping Top, Middle and Bottom peers learn how to master their systemic conditions). More broad avenues of research await.

There is also the possibility of studying culture through the lens of these systemic processes – organizational culture as measured by the characteristic patterns through which these systemic processes are managed; and how different cultural patterns relate to organizational health.

- **Social implications**

OSF has implications for such phenomena as tensions based on differences in race, religion, ethnicity, gender, sexual orientation.[9] The model provides a framework for understanding these tensions, preventing them from developing, or resolving them when they do arise. Again, no systematic research has been done

---

[9] (Oshry 2018) uses the OSF to illuminate our disastrous history of oppression of the 'other'.

in any of these areas. There are also as yet unexplored implications for families as systems and relationships among system members.

- **Consciousness**

Science is based on propositions that can be proven *wrong*. The OSF offers many such propositions, which should make it a rich field for scientific study. Possibly the most challenging feature of OSF are the propositions regarding consciousness:

- that consciousness is not always a reflection of reality – rather it is a consequence of the systemic patterns we have fallen into

- that specific mentalities – Mine, I, and We/Them – are the consequences of specific systemic patterns

- that changing the patterns we have fallen into will change our experiences of self and others

- that changing the patterns will lead to improved outcomes for ourselves, our relationships, and our systems.

It is on these bases that I offer OSF as a prime paradigm candidate.

Does anyone really care about scientific paradigms?

Reflecting on this paper and its likely consequences, I am concerned that some will think that I am disparaging their work. That is not my intention. My purpose is to establish a framework for the *scientific study of organizational systems*. It is my hope that many students of the science of systems life will be stimulated to work with this framework by elaborating it, testing it, developing applications from it.

One measure of the success of this paradigm will be not the number of books it spawns, but the number of research papers. Yet I am also aware of the limitations of a paradigm, as Kuhn says, "Frequently... revolution narrows the scope of a community's professional concerns, increases the extent of its specialization, and attenuates its communication with other groups, both scientific and lay. Though science surely grows in depth, it may not grow in breadth as well." (p.120).

I want to separate science from the rest without disvaluing the rest – the contributions that come to us from intuitions, metaphors, observations in the field, moral convictions, spirituality, connections to other disciplines, synchronistic inspirations (such as the one that brought the Kuhn book and me together), and so forth.

There may be particular concerns for those whose frameworks are challenged and threatened by the Organic Systems Framework, especially those whose careers have been based on the primacy of understanding systems through understanding individuals, those who have put all their eggs in the basket of personality. *A system is not understood by the nature of the characteristics of its parts*. As Fritjof Capra says, "Living systems are integrated wholes whose properties cannot be reduced to those of smaller parts. The essential, or 'systemic,' properties are properties of the whole, which none of the parts have." (1996, p.36.) That fact simply has to be faced. The regular disintegration of 'middle' groups, the coalescence of 'bottom' groups, and the territoriality of 'top' groups has little to do with the character make-up of these systems' individual members; and confronting people on their personal styles or generating norms of authenticity or creating climates of feedback is likely to have limited and at best short-term success. To paraphrase Andrew Salter (1952), it is high time that in matters of understanding social systems the cult of personality, like the elephant of the ancient fable, dragged itself off to some far distant jungle and died. We are not autonomous entities. We are systems creatures. *Our experiences of ourselves, others, our system and other systems, are shaped by the structure and processes of our systems. This fact may be hard for many to accept.*

Finally, there is the question: Who cares? In a field driven by pragmatism and by the need of both practitioners and their gurus to be always on the leading edge, the question of science may be largely irrelevant or, worse, a diversion. Speed. What's the latest? Results. At Power+Systems, my colleagues and I have been conducting seminars and workshops for more than 40 years; and not once has it occurred to us to trumpet the science-base of our work. Who would care? It's results that count. Still, in the ongoing tension between the practical and the theoretical, Kurt Lewin's dictum bears repeating: "There is nothing so practical as a good theory."

Enter Academia

I have been cautioned by a colleague (Lee Bolman, personal communication) against putting too much weight on "bookstore research" while ignoring scholarly work in the field. "Most of the work in bookstores is aimed primarily at managers rather than scholars. The scholars represent another intellectual world that overlaps but is distinct from the stuff written for practitioners. The academics and popularists tend to take little note of one another." Dr. Bolman goes on to point out potential competitors for paradigm status that seem to be getting the most attention in academic circles in recent years: institutional theory, resource-dependence theory, population ecology, transaction-cost theory, and cognitive theory. In the competition for paradigmatic status, the tests are these: Do these theories explain social system phenomena better than other models? Do the theories allow one to predict outcomes? Do they offer improved solutions to existing social problems (If one does X, will Y follow?) Do they open up broad avenues for future research? I have spent much of my time in the field dealing with executives, managers and workers, and I have never heard reference to any of these theories or their applications. It seems reasonable to ask: Where in the world, outside of academia, do these theories show up?

What is unique about OSF is that it is both academic (though not yet sufficiently recognized in academia) and popular. While the theory has been developing, it has concurrently, for over 40 years, been the basis for education about life in organizations in ways that organization members can take specific, theory-based actions to produce specific, theory-based outcomes. The staying power of the theory and its resulting applications – even as other frameworks have come and gone – speak for the power of the paradigm. Naturally, it would be my fondest hope that academicians and, especially, their students would also take a close look at the OSF, for it is in academia that the testing and extension of this framework rightfully belong.

There is a science of social system life and the Organic Systems Framework provides a solid foundation on which system scientists can build – testing, elaborating and applying.

Summary of the Organic Systems Framework

- Human social systems are organic entities interacting with their environments. They are wholes that have properties separate from those of their parts.

- Human systems are patterns of systemic relationships and patterns of systemic processes. Some of these patterns have already been identified; presumably there are more waiting to be identified.

- The identified patterns of relationship and process exist at all levels of systems – family, work group, community, organization, nation, racial/religious/ethnic groups, humanity as a whole.

- Consciousness – that is, how system members experience themselves, others, their system, and other systems – is shaped by the structure and processes of their systems. Bottom system members typically fall into a "We versus Them" mentality; Middle system members fall into separate "I" mentalities; and Top system members fall into territorial "Mine" mentalities.

- System members tend to be blind to the connection between their consciousness and the structure and processes of their systems. As a consequence, members tend to personalize and politicize that which is systemic. This system blindness has resulted in misunderstandings and conflicts among system members; warfare: hot, cold, intra-organizational and cultural; separation and divorce; missed opportunities for productive partnerships; family and organizational disintegration; and such catastrophic disasters as holocausts and ethnic cleansing.

- A paradigm shift from the personal perspective to the Organic Systems Perspective offers the hope of creating saner, healthier, more creative and productive human systems.

References

Regarding the OSF Framework
The OSF paradigm has unfolded over the years in the following publications by the author:

Oshry, Barry (1976a) *Notes on the Power and Systems Perspective*, Power + Systems

_____ (1976b) *Organic Power*, Power + Systems

_____ (1977a) *Controlling the Context of Consciousness*, Power + Systems

_____ (1977b) *Power and Position*, Power + Systems

_____ (1986) *The Possibilities of Organization*, Power + Systems

_____ (1992) *Space Work*, Power + Systems

_____ (1994) *In the Middle*, Power + Systems

_____ (1995) *Seeing Systems*, Berrett-Koehler

_____ (1999) *Leading Systems: Lessons from the Power Lab*, Berrett-Koehler

_____ (2007) *From Relational Blindness to Relational Sight*, Berrett-Koehler

_____ (2017) *Context Context Context*, Triarchy Press

_____ (2018) *Encounters with the "Other"*, Triarchy Press

Regarding the 2000 "Hot Table"
Fisher, Roger and Sharp, Alan (1998) *Getting It Done: How to Lead When You're Not in Charge*, Harper Business

Hammer, Michael (1997) *Beyond Reengineering*, Harper Collins

Heider, John (1986) *The Tao of Leadership,* Humanics

Herman, Stanley M. (1994) *Tao At Work,* Jossey- Bass

Jones, Laurie B. (1996) *Jesus CEO,* Hyperion

Labovits, George and Rosansky, Victor (1997) *The Power of Alignment,* John Wiley

Lee, Blaine (1997) *The Power Principle,* Simon and Schuster

Messing, Bob (1992) *Tao of Management,* Humanics

Nelson, Bob (1997) *1001 Ways to Energize Employees,* Workman

Peters, Tom (1997) *The Circle of Innovation,* Knopf

Pitino, Rick (1997) *Success Is a Choice,* Broadway Books

Roberts, Wess and Ross, Bill (1996) *Make It So: Leadership Lessons from Star Trek,* Hyperion

Senge, Peter (1994) *The Fifth Discipline,* Doubleday

Regarding the text

Capra, Fritjof (1996) *The Web of Life,* Doubleday

Kuhn, Thomas S. (1996) *The Structure of Scientific Revolutions,* 3rd edition, University of Chicago Press

Salter, Andrew (1952) *The Case Against Psychoanalysis,* Henry Holt

About the Author

Barry Oshry is a pioneer in the field of human systems thinking. His life's work has been to empower individuals and organizations by transforming system-blindness into system-sight. The educational programs he has developed include The Power Lab, the Organization Workshop on Creating Partnership, and the When Cultures Meet Workshop.

In 2013 he launched The Worldwide Week of Partnership, during which Power+Systems trainers across the globe conduct pro bono partnership events for educational, charitable, advocacy, and service organizations in their local communities. In 2015 he received a Lifetime Achievement Award from the International Organization Development Network.

Barry is the author of *The Systems Letter*, *Seeing Systems*, *Leading Systems*, *In the Middle*, *The Possibilities of Organization*, and *Context, Context, Context*. He is also a playwright whose stage productions include "What a Way to Make a Living," "Hierarchy," "Power Play," and "Peace."

In 1975 he and his wife and partner, Karen Ellis Oshry, founded Power+Systems, Inc. whose worldwide network of trainers continues the work of empowering individuals and organizations by transforming system-blindness into system-sight. They retired from Power+Systems in 2018.

Barry's latest book is *Context, Context, Context*. See: www.triarchypress.net/context or store.powerandsystems.com

oshrybarry@gmail.com
www.powerandsystems.com
www.worldwideweekofpartnership.org

About the Publisher

Triarchy Press is a small independent publisher of books that bring a wider, systemic or contextual approach to many different areas of life, including:

Government, Education, Health and other public services
Ecology, Sustainability and Regenerative Cultures
Leading and Managing Organizations
Psychotherapy and Arts and other Expressive Therapies
The Money System
Walking, Psychogeography and Mythogeography
Movement and Somatics
Innovation
The Future and Future Studies

For books by Barry Oshry, John Seddon, Nora Bateson, Russ Ackoff, Phil Smith, Bill Tate, Sandra Reeve, Graham Leicester, Alyson Hallett and other remarkable writers, please visit:

www.triarchypress.net

Lightning Source UK Ltd.
Milton Keynes UK
UKHW020231210122
397500UK00009B/138